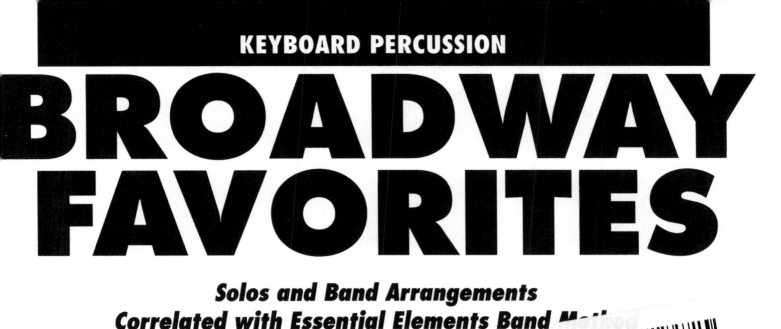

KEYBOARD PERCUSSION

BROADWAY FAVORITES

Solos and Band Arrangements
Correlated with Essential Elements Band Method

Arranged by
MICHAEL SWEENEY

Welcome to Essential Elements Broadway Favorites! There are two versions of each selection in this versatile book. The SOLO version appears in the beginning of each student book. The FULL BAND arrangements of each song follows. The supplemental CD recording or PIANO ACCOMPANIMENT BOOK may be used as an accompaniment for solo performance. Use these recordings when playing solos for friends and family.

ISBN 978-0-7935-9857-1

HAL•LEONARD®
CORPORATION
7777 W. BLUEMOUND RD. P.O. BOX 13819 MILWAUKEE, WI 53213

From Walt Disney's BEAUTY AND THE BEAST: THE BROADWAY MUSICAL

BEAUTY AND THE BEAST

KEYBOARD PERCUSSION
Solo

Lyrics by HOWARD ASHM..
Music by ALAN MENK
Arranged by MICHAEL SWEEN..

From the Musical Production ANNIE

TOMORROW

EYBOARD PERCUSSION
lo

Lyric by MARTIN CHARNIN
Music by CHARLES STROUSE
Arranged by MICHAEL SWEENEY

From the Musical CABARET

CABARET

Words by FRED E...
Music by JOHN KAND...
Arranged by MICHAEL SWEENE...

KEYBOARD PERCUSSION
Solo

From THE SOUND OF MUSIC
EDELWEISS

KEYBOARD PERCUSSION

Lyrics by OSCAR HAMMERSTEIN II
Music by RICHARD RODGERS
Arranged by MICHAEL SWEENEY

From EVITA
DON'T CRY FOR ME ARGENTINA

Words by TIM RICE
Music by ANDREW LLOYD WEBBER
Arranged by MICHAEL SWEENEY

KEYBOARD PERCUSSION
Solo

MCA Music Publishing

GET ME TO THE CHURCH ON TIME

KEYBOARD PERCUSSION

Words by ALAN JAY LERNER
Music by FREDERICK LOEWE
Arranged by MICHAEL SWEENEY

60051

From LES MISÉRABLES

I DREAMED A DREAM

Music by CLAUDE-MICHEL SCHÖNBER
Lyrics by ALAIN BOUBLI
JEAN-MARC NATEL and HERBERT KRETZME
Arranged by MICHAEL SWEEN

KEYBOARD PERCUSSION
Solo

GO GO GO JOSEPH

KEYBOARD PERCUSSION
Solo

Music by ANDREW LLOYD WEBBER
Lyrics by TIM RICE
Arranged by MICHAEL SWEENEY

860051

From CATS
MEMORY

KEYBOARD PERCUSSION
Solo

Music by ANDREW LLOYD WEBBER
Text by TREVOR NUNN after T.S. ELIOT
Arranged by MICHAEL SWEENEY

THE PHANTOM OF THE OPERA

KEYBOARD PERCUSSION

Music by ANDREW LLOYD WEBBER
Lyrics by CHARLES HART
Additional Lyrics by RICHARD STILGOE and MIKE BATT
Arranged by MICHAEL SWEENEY

360051

From Meredith Willson's THE MUSIC MAN

SEVENTY SIX TROMBONES

By MEREDITH WILLSON
Arranged by MICHAEL SWEENEY

KEYBOARD PERCUSSION
Solo

BEAUTY AND THE BEAST

KEYBOARD PERCUSSION
Band Arrangement

Lyrics by HOWARD ASHMAN
Music by ALAN MENKEN
Arranged by MICHAEL SWEENEY

From the Musical Production ANNIE
TOMORROW

KEYBOARD PERCUSSION
Band Arrangement

Lyric by MARTIN CHARN
Music by CHARLES STROU
Arranged by MICHAEL SWEEN

CABARET

KEYBOARD PERCUSSION
Band Arrangement

Words by FRED EBB
Music by JOHN KANDER
Arranged by MICHAEL SWEENEY

From THE SOUND OF MUSIC
EDELWEISS

KEYBOARD PERCUSSION
Band Arrangement

Lyrics by OSCAR HAMMERSTEIN
Music by RICHARD RODGERS
Arranged by MICHAEL SWEENEY

From EVITA
DON'T CRY FOR ME ARGENTINA

KEYBOARD PERCUSSION
Band Arrangement

Words by TIM RICE
Music by ANDREW LLOYD WEBBER
Arranged by MICHAEL SWEENEY

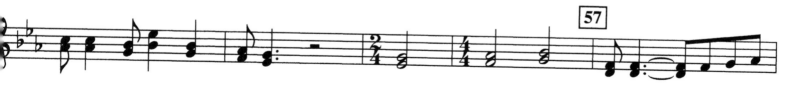

From MY FAIR LADY

GET ME TO THE CHURCH ON TIME

KEYBOARD PERCUSSION
Band Arrangement

Words by ALAN JAY LERNER
Music by FREDERICK LOEWE
Arranged by MICHAEL SWEENEY

From LES MISÉRABLES
I DREAMED A DREAM

YBOARD PERCUSSION
d Arrangement

Music by CLAUDE-MICHEL SCHÖNBERG
Lyrics by ALAIN BOUBLIL,
JEAN-MARC NATEL and HERBERT KRETZMER
Arranged by MICHAEL SWEENEY

Gently

Bells

60051

From JOSEPH AND THE AMAZING TECHNICOLOR DREAMCOAT

GO GO GO JOSEPH

Music by ANDREW LLOYD WEBBER
Lyrics by TIM RICE
Arranged by MICHAEL SWEENEY

KEYBOARD PERCUSSION
Band Arrangement
(Bells, Shaker)

00860051

From CATS
MEMORY

KEYBOARD PERCUSSION
Band Arrangement

Music by ANDREW LLOYD WEBBER
Text by TREVOR NUNN after T.S. ELIOT
Arranged by MICHAEL SWEENEY

60051

From THE PHANTOM OF THE OPERA

THE PHANTOM OF THE OPERA

KEYBOARD PERCUSSION
Band Arrangement

Music by ANDREW LLOYD WEBBER
Lyrics by CHARLES HART
Additional Lyrics by RICHARD STILGOE and MIKE BATT
Arranged by MICHAEL SWEENEY

From Meredith Willson's THE MUSIC MAN

SEVENTY SIX TROMBONES

By MEREDITH WILLSON
Arranged by MICHAEL SWEENEY

KEYBOARD PERCUSSION
2nd Arrangement

60051